100 POEMS TO HELP YOU SLEEP

To Matilda, Tabitha and all cats,
to whom sleep is so important, with all my love.

100 POEMS TO HELP YOU SLEEP

EDITED BY JANE MCMORLAND HUNTER

BATSFORD

Introduction

One of my fondest memories of childhood were the outings we called the Night-Nights. Looking back I suspect they were merely a detour when we went to collect eggs from the nearby farm and probably only happened once a week but, in my mind, they were an almost nightly occurrence where we drove slowly round the countryside saying goodnight. After collecting the eggs we visited the horses and then two huge bulls, Monty and George. We collected wild flowers, waved at train drivers and watched the sunset. It was the perfect end to the day. Now I often recreate that sense of calm by reading a poem.

Since ancient times, poetry has been renowned for its healing qualities and the aim of this collection of poetry is to gently guide you into a mood for sleep. It is deliberately not divided into chapters so the reader can work their way straight through or dip in at random. However I have arranged the poems in a loose order which moves from early evening through twilight and dusk with lullabies leading towards night with the moon and stars. Then there are poems on sleep and dreams and finally a section on general contentment. They span the breadth of the world over five hundred years and include the obvious pieces as well as lesser-known works which I hope will surprise and delight.

In an ideal world, evening marks the moment when the work of the day is done and it is time to go home. The natural world also settles with day birds returning to their nests and animals to their dens or lairs. Many poets reflect on the passing of a satisfactory day, looking at the lives of shepherds and farm-workers and, although I suspect these lives may be seen through rose-tinted spectacles, they create an image of calm and well-earned rest.

At some point in the evening it becomes twilight, possibly my favourite word in the English language. Technically, this is the time when the sun is below the horizon but its rays still, partially, illuminate the atmosphere. This scientific definition is of little concern here; thanks to poetry we have a god of evening leaning out of a band of dull gold (D. H. Lawrence), a spirit from diviner air sensed by Ethelwyn Wetherald and a time that creeps wearing shadowy garments as glimpsed by E. Pauline Johnson, also known as Tekahionwake.

In childhood we are read lullabies to calm us in the evening and send us to sleep. Why, as adults, should we not continue this delightful practice? Some here are aimed at children, others look from a more adult perspective. Half past eight seems a crucial time – do we go up the stairs unwillingly or of our own choice?

The night is a time for sleep but much of the world is more beautiful in the dark and some of the poems in this collection celebrate, rather than fear, wakefulness. Stars, whether real or in the form of fireflies, and the moon and its magical light more than make up for a little lost sleep. All these have scientific explanations but there is a time when one should ignore the learned astronomers and follow Walt Whitman, enjoy the night-air and simply marvel at the stars and moon.

Counting sheep may be the traditional way to encourage sleep but here watching sport, lying amongst wild flowers, enjoying solitude or the comfort of a lover are all recommended. My favourite suggestion is that of Roger Robinson: keep a portable Paradise in your pocket, which you can take out and release wherever you are. By day we are often shackled to duty but night is the time when our spirits can roam free. According to E. Nesbit, night has a kindlier heart: 'Day keeps us prisoned close but Night / Lifts off Day's chains'. The ghosts of the night have the power to terrify but the ones here are benign, those that wander by the wizard oak or fairy stream of William Motherwell must surely be kind. Dreams too are gentle here and never descend into nightmares. They allow us to be together with lost ones with no fear of separation, allow our wildest fancies to wander free and, in the wonderful words of Sara Teasdale, allow us to love and sleep at the same time.

Midnight is the turning point of each day, a moment most of us miss but it gives us a new chance ''Tis the hour of endings, ended / Of beginnings unbegun' (Louisa Bevington) and, for Nikita Gill there is magic at midnight, a chance for us to mend, restore and recover all we thought was lost.

The final poems focus on contentment, the ability to find peace and calm regardless of age, creed or situation. Whatever we have done or how the day has left us, sleep should bring rest and recuperation so we are ready for a new, and, if necessary, better day. Gently unwinding, casting off the cares of the day and preparing ourselves for sleep with a poem is the perfect way to enjoy the evening and ensure that one is prepared for a good night's sleep.

The Evening Sun

The evening sun was sinking down
On low green hills and clustered trees
It was a scene as fair and lone
As ever felt the soothing breeze

That bends the grass when day is gone
And gives the wave a brighter blue
And makes the soft white clouds sail on
Like spirits of eternal dew

Which all the morn had hovered o'er
The azure flowers where they were nursed
And now return to heaven once more
Where their bright glories shone at first

Emily Brontë (1818-1848)

'the stars are out, Twinkling all the sky about'

Starlight
Lucy Larcom

When on the Marge of Evening

When on the marge of evening the last blue light is
    broken,
And winds of dreamy odour are loosened from afar,
Or when my lattice opens, before the lark hath
    spoken,
On dim laburnum-blossoms, and morning's dying
    star,

I think of thee (O mine the more if other eyes be
    sleeping!),
Whose greater noonday splendours the many share
    and see,
While sacred and for ever, some perfect law is
    keeping
The late, the early twilight, alone and sweet for me.

Louise Imogen Guiney (1861–1920)

Autumn Evening

I love to hear the evening crows go bye
And see the starnels darken down the sky
The bleaching stack the bustling sparrow leaves
And plops with merry note beneath the eaves
The odd and lated pigeon bounces bye
As if a wary watching hawk was nigh
While far and fearing nothing high and slow
The stranger birds to distant places go
While short of flight the evening robin comes
To watch the maiden sweeping out the crumbs
Nor fears the idle shout of passing boy
But pecks about the door and sings for joy
Then in the hovel where the cows are fed
Finds till the morning comes a pleasant bed

John Clare (1793-1864)

Evening
From *A Summer Day*

Now weary labourers perceive, well-pleased,
The shadows lengthen, and the oppressive day
With all its toil fast wearing to an end.
The sun, far in the west, with sidelong beam
Plays on the yellow head of the round haycock,
And fields are checkered with fantastic shapes
Or tree, or shrub, or gate, or rugged stone,
All lengthened out, in antic disproportion,
Upon the darkened grass.–
They finish out their long and toilsome task.
Then, gathering up their rakes and scattered coats,
With the less cumbrous fragments of their feast,
Return right gladly to their peaceful homes.

Joanna Baillie (1762–1851)

Sunset

There is a band of dull gold in the west, and say
  what you like
again and again some god of evening leans out of it
and shares being with me, silkily
all of twilight.

D. H. Lawrence (1885–1930)

'The shadows now so long do grow'

Evening Quatrains
Charles Cotton

The sun is verging to the sea
From *Beachy Head*

For now the sun is verging to the sea,
And as he westward sinks, the floating clouds
Suspended, move upon the evening gale,
And gathering round his orb, as if to shade
The insufferable brightness, they resign
Their gauzy whiteness; and more warmed, assume
All hues of purple. There, transparent gold
Mingles with ruby tints, and sapphire gleams,
And colours, such as nature through her works
Shows only in the ethereal canopy.

Charlotte Smith (1749–1806)

Calm is the fragrant air

Calm is the fragrant air, and loth to lose
Day's grateful warmth, tho' moist with falling dews.
Look for the stars, you'll say that there are none;
Look up a second time, and, one by one,
You mark them twinkling out with silvery light,
And wonder how they could elude the sight!
The birds, of late so noisy in their bowers,
Warbled a while with faint and fainter powers,
But now are silent as the dim-seen flowers:
Nor does the village Church-clock's iron tone
The time's and season's influence disown;
Nine beats distinctly to each other bound
In drowsy sequence – how unlike the sound
That, in rough winter, oft inflicts a fear
On fireside listeners, doubting what they hear!
The shepherd, bent on rising with the sun,
Had closed his door before the day was done,
And now with thankful heart to bed doth creep,
And joins his little children in their sleep
The bat, lured forth where trees the lane o'ershade,
Flits and reflits along the close arcade;

The busy dor-hawk chases the white moth
With burring note, which Industry and Sloth
Might both be pleased with, for it suits them both.
A stream is heard – I see it not, but know
By its soft music whence the waters flow:
Wheels and the tread of hoofs are heard no more;
One boat there was, but it will touch the shore
With the next dipping of its slackened oar;
Faint sound, that, for the gayest of the gay,
Might give to serious thought a moment's sway,
As a last token of man's toilsome day!

William Wordsworth (1780-1850)

A Summer Eve's Vision
Verses 1-3

Thought from the bosom's inmost cell,
  By magic tints made visible.
            Montgomery.

I heard last night a lovely lute,
  I heard it in the sunset hour,
When every jarring sound was mute,
  And golden light bathed field and flower.

I saw the hills in bright repose,
  And far away a silent sea,
Whilst nearer hamlet-homes arose,
  Each sheltered by its guardian tree.

O'er all was spread a soft blue sky,
  And where the distant waters rolled,
Type of the blest abodes on high
  Swept the sun's path of pearl and gold.

Maria Jane Jewsbury (1800–1833)

'The evening sun was sinking down'

At Dusk
Emily Brontë

Evening Quatrains

I

The day's grown old, the fainting sun
Has but a little way to run,
And yet his steeds, with all his skill,
Scarce lug the chariot down the hill.

II

With labour spent, and thirst opprest,
Whilst they strain hard to gain the west,
From fetlocks hot drops melted light,
Which turn to meteors in the night.

III

The shadows now so long do grow,
That brambles like tall cedars show,
Mole-hills seem mountains, and the ant
Appears a monstrous elephant.

IV

A very little, little flock
Shades thrice the ground that it would stock;
Whilst the small stripling following them
Appears a mighty Polypheme.

V

These being brought into the fold,
And by the thrifty master told,
He thinks his wages are well paid,
Since none are either lost or stray'd.

VI

Now lowing herds are each-where heard,
Chains rattle in the villien's yard,
The cart's on tail set down to rest,
Bearing on high the cuckold's crest.

VII

The hedge is stripped, the clothes brought in,
Nought's left without should be within,
The bees are hiv'd, and hum their charm,
Whilst every house does seem a swarm.

VIII

The cock now to the roost is prest:
For he must call up all the rest;
The sow's fast pegg'd within the sty,
To still her squeaking progeny.

IX

Each one has had his supping mess,
The cheese is put into the press,
The pans and bowls are scalded all,
Rear'd up against the milk-house wall.

X

And now on benches all are sat
In the cool air to sit and chat,
Till Phoebus, dipping in the west,
Shall lead the world the way to rest.

Charles Cotton (1630–1687)

In the Evening

But in the evening
When the sun seeks rest
I evaporate . . . I become
Its wind

And remind us of the songs
That tell the history
Of the comfort and Love
So that the Children
May know

Nikki Giovanni (1943–)

'blissfull
dreams
may
then
arise'

Night
Anne Brontë

At Dusk

The phantom time of day is here.
  Some spirit from diviner air
Unto our blindness draweth near,
  And in our musing seems to share.

Who hath not in a darkening wood
  At twilight's moment dimly known
That all his hurts were understood
  By some near presence not his own;

That all his griefs were comforted,
  His aspirations given release;
And that upon his troubled head
  Was laid the viewless hand of Peace

Too sure for doubt, too sweet for fear,
  Unfelt in days of toil and stress;
But when the twilight brings it near
  Who hath not felt its tenderness?

Ethelwyn Wetherald (1857-1940)

Twilight

Grey the sky, and growing dimmer,
  And the twilight lulls the sea;
Half in vagueness, half in glimmer,
  Nature shrouds her mystery.

What have all the hours been spent for?
  Why the on and on of things?
Why eternity's procession
  Of the days and evenings?

Hours of sunshine, hours of gleaming,
  Wing their unexplaining flight,
With a measured punctuation
  Of unconsciousness, at night.

Just at sunset, was translucence,
  When the west was all aflame;
So I asked the sea a question,
  And an answer nearly came.

Is there nothing but Occurrence?
  Though each detail seem an Act,
Is that whole we deem so pregnant
  But unemphasized Fact?

Or, when dusk is in the hollows
  Of the hill-side and the wave,
Are things just so much in earnest
  That they cannot but be grave?

Nay, the lesson of the Twilight
  Is as simple as 'tis deep;
Acquiescence, acquiescence,
  And the coming on of sleep.

Louisa S. Bevington (1845-1895)

'Into the golden land of dreams'

Last night as I lay gazing
with shut eyes
Henry David Thoreau

Sowing

It was a perfect day
For sowing; just
As sweet and dry was the ground
As tobacco-dust.

I tasted deep the hour
Between the far
Owl's chuckling first soft cry
And the first star.

A long stretched hour it was;
Nothing undone
Remained; the early seeds
All safely sown.

And now, hark at the rain,
Windless and light,
Half a kiss, half a tear,
Saying good-night.

Edward Thomas (1878–1917)

Down to Sleep

November woods are bare and still;
   November days are clear and bright;
Each noon burns up the morning's chill;
   The morning's snow is gone by night;
   Each day my steps grow slow, grow light,
As through the woods I reverent creep,
Watching all things lie "down to sleep."

I never knew before what beds,
   Fragrant to smell, and soft to touch,
The forest sifts and shapes and spreads;
   I never knew before how much
   Of human sound there is in such
Low tones as through the forest sweep
When all wild things lie "down to sleep."

Each day I find new coverlids
    Tucked in, and more sweet eyes shut tight;
Sometimes the viewless mother bids
    Her ferns kneel down, full in my sight;
    I hear their chorus of "good-night;"
And half I smile, and half I weep,
Listening while they lie "down to sleep."

November woods are bare and still;
    November days are bright and good;
Life's noon burns up life's morning chill;
    Life's night rests feet which long have stood;
    Some warm soft bed, in field or wood,
The mother will not fail to keep,
Where we can "lay us down to sleep."

Helen Hunt Jackson (1830-1885)

'sleep
and rest,
sleep
and rest'

Sweet and Low
Alfred, Lord Tennyson

Hymn to the Evening

Soon as the sun forsook the eastern main
The pealing thunder shook the heavenly plain;
Majestic grandeur! From the zephyr's wing,
Exhales the incense of the blooming spring,
Soft purl the streams, the birds renew their notes,
And through the air their mingled music floats.

Through all the heavens what beauteous dyes are
    spread,
But the west glories in the deepest red:
So may our breasts with ev'ry virtue glow,
The living temples of our God below!

Filled with the praise of him who gives the light,
And draws the sable curtains of the night,
Let placid slumbers soothe each weary mind,
At morn to wake more heavenly, more refined;
So shall the labors of the day begin
More pure, more guarded from the snares of sin.
Night's leaden sceptre seals my drowsy eyes,
Then cease, my song, till fair Aurora rise.

Phillis Wheatley (1753–1784)

Night
From *Songs of Innocence*

The sun descending in the west,
The evening star does shine;
The birds are silent in their nest,
And I must seek for mine.
The moon, like a flower
In heaven's high bower,
With silent delight,
Sits and smiles on the night.

Farewell, green fields and happy groves,
Where flocks have took delight,
Where lambs have nibbled, silent moves
The feet of angels bright;
Unseen, they pour blessing,
And joy without ceasing,
On each bud and blossom,
And each sleeping bosom.

They look in every thoughtless nest
Where birds are cover'd warm;
They visit caves of every beast,
To keep them all from harm:
If they see any weeping
That should have been sleeping,
They pour sleep on their head,
And sit down by their bed.

When wolves and tigers howl for prey,
They pitying stand and weep;
Seeking to drive their thirst away,
And keep them from the sheep.
But if they rush dreadful,
The angels, most heedful,
Receive each mild spirit,
New worlds to inherit.

And there the lion's ruddy eyes
Shall flow with tears of gold:
And pitying the tender cries,
And walking round the fold:
Saying: 'Wrath by His meekness,
And, by His health, sickness,
Is driven away
From our immortal day.

'And now beside thee, bleating lamb,
I can lie down and sleep,
Or think on Him who bore thy name,
Graze after thee, and weep.
For, wash'd in life's river,
My bright mane for ever
Shall shine like the gold,
As I guard o'er the fold.'

William Blake (1757–1827)

'Midnight's all a glimmer'

The Lake Isle of Innisfree
W. B. Yeats

Nightfall

She sits beside: through four low panes of glass
The sun, a misty meadow, and the stream;
Falling through rounded elms the last sunbeam.
Through night's thick fibre sudden barges pass
With great forelights of gold, with trailing mass
Of timber: rearward of their transient gleam
The shadows settle, and profounder dream
Enters, fulfils the shadows. Vale and grass
Are now no more; a last leaf strays about,
Then every wandering ceases; we remain.
Clear dusk, the face of wind is on the sky:
The eyes I love lift to the upper pane –
Their voice gives note of welcome quietly
'I love the air in which the stars come out.'

Katherine Bradley (1846-1914) and Edith Cooper (1862-1913)
writing as Michael Field

Meeting at Night

I

The grey sea and the long black land;
And the yellow half-moon large and low;
And the startled little waves that leap
In fiery ringlets from their sleep,
As I gain the cove with pushing prow,
And quench its speed in the slushy sand.

II

Then a mile of warm sea-scented beach;
Three fields to cross till a farm appears;
A tap at the pane, the quick sharp scratch
And blue spurt of a lighted match,
And a voice less loud, thro' its joys and fears,
Than the two hearts beating each to each!

Robert Browning (1812–1889)

My Bed is a Boat

My bed is like a little boat;
   Nurse helps me in when I embark;
She girds me in my sailor's coat
   And starts me in the dark.

At night, I go on board and say
   Good-night to all my friends on shore;
I shut my eyes and sail away
   And see and hear no more.

And sometimes things to bed I take,
   As prudent sailors have to do;
Perhaps a slice of wedding-cake,
   Perhaps a toy or two.

All night across the dark we steer;
   But when the day returns at last,
Safe in my room, beside the pier,
   I find my vessel fast.

Robert Louis Stevenson (1850–1894)

Half Past Eight

Creaking stairs and bed for me –
For lucky ones somewhere
A curtain of light goes sliding up,
And Peter Pan is there.

Somewhere the other children see
Hook and his pirate band
Seeking the Lost Boys snugly hid
In the Never, Never Land.
Others will save poor Tinker Bell,
And I not there to help;
When Peter pipes from his tree-top house
He'll not pipe to myself!

If wishes did all they ought to do
Things would not be this way –
Those other children would go to bed,
And I would be at the play.

Rachel Field (1894-1942)

Grown-up

Was it for this I uttered prayers,
And sobbed and cursed and kicked the stairs,
That now, domestic as a plate,
I should retire at half-past eight?

Edna St Vincent Millay (1892–1950)

Lullaby

Golden slumbers kisse your eyes,
Smiles awake you when you rise;
Sleepe, pretty wantons, do not cry,
And I will sing a lullabie,
Rocke them, rocke them, lullabie.

Care is heavie, therefore sleepe you,
You are care, and care must keep you;
Sleepe pretty wantons, do not cry,
And I will sing a lullabie,
Rocke them, rocke them, lullabie.

Thomas Dekker (c. 1572–1632)

'now
with
thankful
heart
to bed'

Calm is the fragrant air
William Wordsworth

After Sunset
Lines 1-12

Rest – *rest* – four little letters, one short word,
Enfolding an infinitude of bliss –
Rest is upon the earth. The heavy clouds
Hang poised in silent ether, motionless,
Seeking nor sun nor breeze. No restless star
Thrills the sky's gray-robed breast with pulsing rays,
The night's heart has throbb'd out.
          No grass blade stirs,
No downy-wingèd moth comes flittering by
Caught by the light – Thank God, there is no light,
No open-eyed, loud-voiced, quick motion'd light,
Nothing but gloom and rest.

Dinah Maria Craik (1826–1887)

Lullaby

Lay your sleeping head, my love,
Human on my faithless arm;
Time and fevers burn away
Individual beauty from
Thoughtful children, and the grave
Proves the child ephemeral:
But in my arms till break of day
Let the living creature lie,
Mortal, guilty, but to me
The entirely beautiful.

Soul and body have no bounds:
To lovers as they lie upon
Her tolerant enchanted slope
In their ordinary swoon,
Grave the vision Venus sends
Of supernatural sympathy,
Universal love and hope;
While an abstract insight wakes
Among the glaciers and the rocks
The hermit's carnal ecstasy.

Certainty, fidelity
On the stroke of midnight pass
Like vibrations of a bell,
And fashionable madmen raise
Their pedantic boring cry:
Every farthing of the cost,
All the dreaded cards foretell,
Shall be paid, but from this night
Not a whisper, not a thought,
Not a kiss nor look be lost.

Beauty, midnight, vision dies:
Let the winds of dawn that blow
Softly round your dreaming head
Such a day of welcome show
Eye and knocking heart may bless,
Find the mortal world enough;
Noons of dryness find you fed
By the involuntary powers,
Nights of insult let you pass
Watched by every human love.

W. H. Auden (1907-1973)

The Beautiful Land of Nod

Come, cuddle your head on my shoulder, dear,
    Your head like the golden-rod,
And we will go sailing away from here
    To the beautiful Land of Nod.
Away from life's hurry, and flurry, and worry,
    Away from earth's shadows and gloom,
To a world of fair weather we'll float off together,
    Where roses are always in bloom.

Just shut up your eyes, and fold your hands,
    Your hands like the leaves of a rose,
And we will go sailing to those fair lands
    That never an atlas shows.
On the North and the West they are bounded by rest,
    On the South and the East, by dreams;
'Tis the country ideal, where nothing is real,
    But everything only seems.

Just drop down the curtains of your dear eyes,
    Those eyes like a bright blue-bell,
And we will sail out under starlit skies,
    To the land where the fairies dwell.
Down the river of sleep, our barque shall sweep,
    Till it reaches that mystical Isle
Which no man hath seen, but where all have been,
    And there we will pause awhile.

I will croon you a song as we float along,
    To that shore that is blessed of God,
Then, ho! for that fair land, we're off for that rare
    land,
    That beautiful Land of Nod.

Ella Wheeler Wilcox (1850–1919)

The Fairies Sing
From *A Midsummer Night's Dream*, Act II, scene ii

You spotted snakes with double tongue,
Thorny hedgehogs, be not seen.
Newts and blindworms, do no wrong,
Come not near our fairy queen.

Chorus:
Philomel, with melody
Sing in our sweet lullaby.
Lulla, lulla, lullaby, lulla, lulla, lullaby.
Never harm, Nor spell nor charm
Come our lovely lady nigh.
So good night, with lullaby.

Weaving spiders, come not here;
Hence, you long-legg'd spinners, hence!
Beetles black, approach not near.
Worm nor snail, do no offence.

Chorus:
  Philomel, with melody
  Sing in our sweet lullaby.
Lulla, lulla, lullaby, lulla, lulla, lullaby.
  Never harm, Nor spell nor charm
  Come our lovely lady nigh.
  So good night, with lullaby.

Hence, away! Now all is well.

William Shakespeare (1564–1616)

'the
twilight
lulls
the sea'

Twilight
Louisa S Bevington

O! once again good night!

O! once again good night!
And be thy slumbers light,
Pleasant thy dreams and bright
  As sun-clad mist; −
And when they disappear,
O! may thy mind be clear
From every doubt and fear
  As lake by breezes kist!

Sara Coleridge (1802–1852)

Matthew, Mark, Luke and John

Matthew, Mark, Luke and John,
Bless the bed that I lie on.
 Four corners to my bed,
 Four angels round my head;
 One to watch and one to pray
 And two to bear my soul away.

Anon

Sweet and Low
From *The Princess III*

Sweet and low, sweet and low,
    Wind of the western sea,
Low, low, breathe and blow,
    Wind of the western sea!
Over the rolling waters go,
Come from the dying moon, and blow,
    Blow him again to me;
While my little one, while my pretty one, sleeps.

Sleep and rest, sleep and rest,
    Father will come to thee soon;
Rest, rest, on mother's breast,
    Father will come to thee soon;
Father will come to his babe in the nest,
Silver sails all out of the west
    Under the silver moon:
Sleep, my little one, sleep, my pretty one, sleep.

Alfred, Lord Tennyson (1809–1892)

A Dutch Lullaby

Wynken, Blynken, and Nod one night
   Sailed off in a wooden shoe,–
Sailed on a river of crystal light
   Into a sea of dew.
"Where are you going, and what do you wish?"
   The old moon asked the three.
"We have come to fish for the herring-fish
   That live in this beautiful sea;
   Nets of silver and gold have we,"
      Said Wynken,
      Blynken,
      And Nod.

The old moon laughed and sang a song,
   As they rocked in the wooden shoe;
And the wind that sped them all night long
   Ruffled the waves of dew;
The little stars were the herring-fish
   That lived in the beautiful sea.
"Now cast your nets wherever you wish,–
   Never afraid are we!"
   So cried the stars to the fishermen three,
      Wynken,
      Blynken,
      And Nod.

All night long their nets they threw
   To the stars in the twinkling foam,—
Then down from the skies came the wooden shoe,
   Bringing the fishermen home:
'Twas all so pretty a sail, it seemed
   As if it could not be;
And some folk thought 'twas a dream they'd dreamed
   Of sailing that beautiful sea;
   But I shall name you the fishermen three:
      Wynken,
      Blynken,
      And Nod.

Wynken and Blynken are two little eyes,
   And Nod is a little head,
And the wooden shoe that sailed the skies
   Is a wee one's trundle-bed;
So shut your eyes while Mother sings
   Of wonderful sights that be,
And you shall see the beautiful things
   As you rock in the misty sea
   Where the old shoe rocked the fishermen three:—
      Wynken,
      Blynken,
      And Nod.

Eugene Field (1850–1895)

The Birds' Lullaby

I

Sing to us, cedars; the twilight is creeping
  With shadowy garments, the wilderness through;
All day we have carolled, and now would be sleeping,
  So echo the anthems we warbled to you;
      While we swing, swing,
      And your branches sing,
      And we drowse to your dreamy whispering.

II

Sing to us, cedars; the night-wind is sighing,
  Is wooing, is pleading, to hear you reply;
And here in your arms we are restfully lying,
  And longing to dream to your soft lullaby;
      While we swing, swing,
      And your branches sing.
      And we drowse to your dreamy whispering.

III

Sing to us, cedars; your voice is so lowly,
  Your breathing so fragrant, your branches so
    strong;
Our little nest-cradles are swaying so slowly,
  While zephyrs are breathing their slumberous song.
      And we swing, swing,
      While your branches sing,
      And we drowse to your dreamy whispering.

E. Pauline Johnson / Tekahionwake (1862–1913)

'I shut
my eyes
and sail
away'

My Bed is a Boat
Robert Louis Stevenson

Prayer for a Child

Bless this milk and bless this bread.
Bless this soft and waiting bed
Where I presently shall be
Wrapped in sweet security.
Through the darkness, through the night
Let no danger come to fright
My sleep till morning once again
Beckons at the window pane.
Bless the toys whose shapes I know,
The shoes that take me to and fro
Up and down and everywhere.
Bless my little painted chair.
Bless the lamplight, bless the fire,
Bless the hands that never tire
In their loving care of me.
Bless my friends and family.
Bless my Father and my Mother
And keep us close to one another.
Bless other children, near and far,
And keep them safe and free from fear.
So let me sleep and let me wake
In peace and health, for Jesus' sake.

AMEN

Rachel Field (1894–1942)

Lullaby

Beloved, may your sleep be sound
That have found it where you fed.
What were all the world's alarms
To mighty Paris when he found
Sleep upon a golden bed
That first dawn in Helen's arms?

Sleep, beloved, such a sleep
As did that wild Tristram know
When, the potion's work being done,
Roe could run or doe could leap
Under oak and beechen bough,
Roe could leap or doe could run;

Such a sleep and sound as fell
Upon Eurotas' grassy bank
When the holy bird, that there
Accomplished his predestined will,
From the limbs of Leda sank
But not from her protecting care.

W. B. Yeats (1865–1930)

Sleeping Sea

Sleeping sea, how calm you seem,
This night without breeze:
Your dreams are waves,
Lapping on shores of shingle,
In slow, somniferous ebb and flow.
And looking down,
The moon observes her opal face
In scattered fragments on the surface,
As if through a glass darkly.
Oh, the inky depths dwell
Never more so in the realms of myth
Than in the hush of indigo,
Where whispered stories
Carried forth on tides from long ago,
Are rocked in cradles,
And in storm-worn boats.
And the sea's *berceuse*,
Lulls, with soulful sighs
And soothing verse,
In rageless waters,
Far from the foreboding swell;
Each shallow breath,
Barely a wrinkle in time,
Yet ceaselessly eternal and divine.

Jana Synková (1968–)

Summer Night Piece

The garden is steeped in moonlight,
Full to its high edges with brimming silver,
And the fish-ponds brim and darken
And run in little serpent lights soon extinguished.
Lily-pads lie upon the surface, beautiful as the
  tarnishings on frail old silver,
And the Harvest moon droops heavily out of the sky,
A ripe, white melon, intensely, magnificently, shining.
Your window is orange in the moonlight,
It glows like a lamp behind the branches of the old
  wistaria,
It burns like a lamp before a shrine,
The small, intimate, familiar shrine
Placed reverently among the bricks
Of a much-loved garden wall.

Amy Lowell (1874-1825)

'be thy
slumbers
light,
pleasant
thy dreams'

O! once again good night!
Sara Coleridge

The Evening Star

Thou fair-hair'd angel of the evening,
Now, whilst the sun rests on the mountains, light
Thy bright torch of love; thy radiant crown
Put on, and smile upon our evening bed!
Smile on our loves, and while thou drawest the
Blue curtains of the sky, scatter thy silver dew
On every flower that shuts its sweet eyes
In timely sleep. Let thy west wind sleep on
The lake; speak silence with thy glimmering eyes,
And wash the dusk with silver. Soon, full soon,
Dost thou withdraw; then the wolf rages wide,
And then the lion glares thro' the dun forest:
The fleeces of our flocks are cover'd with
Thy sacred dew: protect them with thine influence.

William Blake (1757–1827)

Day and Night

Night, ambushed in the darkling wood,
    Waited to seize the sleeping field,
His sentinels the pine trees stood
    Till the sun fell beneath his shield.
Then when the day at last was dead,
    Night, in his might, marched conquering.
Across the land his banner spread,
    And reigned as victor and as King.

And you and I – all days apart
    Rejoiced to see Night's victory,
Because he has a kindlier heart
    Than Day wears with his sovereignty:
Day keeps us prisoned close, but Night
    Lifts off Day's chains, and all night through
You dream of me, my life's delight,
    And all night through I dream of you.

E. Nesbit (1858–1924)

O Love You So Fear the Dark

O love, you so fear the dark
you so accustomed to fighting.
It only seems like the night
but it's a veiled overture to light
It is transitory love, it is passing.
The dagger, love, sheath it.

The bloodied dove, love, release it.
There is nothing to fear
It is dark only as your eyes
or my hair
and it is kind love
It leads to light
If you but knew it
Only unarmed will you go through it.

Lorna Goodison (1947–)

Hymn to Diana
From *Cynthias Revells*

Queene and huntresse, chaste and faire,
   Now the Sunne is laid to sleepe,
Seated in thy silver chaire,
   State in wonted manner keepe:
Hesperus intreats thy light,
Goddesse, excellently bright.

Earth, let not thy envious shade
   Dare it selfe to interpose;
Cynthia's shining orb was made
   Heaven to cleere, when day did close:
Blesse us then with wished sight,
Goddesse, excellently bright.

Lay thy bow of pearle apart,
   And thy crystall-shining quiver;
Give unto the flying hart
   Space to breathe, how short soever;
Thou that mak'st a day of night,
Goddesse, excellently bright.

Ben Jonson (1572–1637)

'There shall be no night there'
(In the Fields)

Across these wind-blown meadows I can see
  The far off glimmer of the little town,
  And feel the darkness slowly shutting down
To lock from day's long glare my soul and me.
  Then through my blood the coming mystery
Of night steals to my heart and turns my feet
Toward that chamber in the lamp-lit street,
  Where waits the pillow of thy breast and thee.

'There shall be no night there' – no curtained pane
  To shroud love's speechlessness and loose thy hair
For kisses swift and sweet as falling rain.
  No soft release of life – no evening prayer.
  Nor shall we waking greet the dawn, aware
That with the darkness we may sleep again.

Charlotte Mew (1869–1928)

A Nocturnal Reverie
Lines 1–17

In such a night, when every tender wind
Is to its distant cavern safe confined;
And gentle Philomel, still waking, sings;
Or from some tree, famed for the owl's delight,
She, hollowing clear, directs the wand'rer right:
In such a night, when passing clouds give place,
Or thinly veil the heaven's mysterious face;
When in some river, overhung with green,
The waving moon and the trembling leaves are seen;
When freshened grass now bears itself upright,
And makes cool banks to pleasing rest invite,
Whence springs the woodbind, and the bramble-rose,
And where the sleepy cowslip sheltered grows;
Whilst now a paler hue the foxglove takes,
Yet chequers still with red the dusky brakes
When scattered glow-worms, but in twilight fine,
Shew trivial beauties, watch their hour to shine.

Anne Finch (1661–1720)

Moonrise

I awoke in the Midsummer not to call night, |
  in the white and the walk of the morning:
The moon, dwindled and thinned to the fringe |
  of a finger-nail held to the candle,
Or paring of paradisaïcal fruit, | lovely in waning
  but lustreless,
Stepped from the stool, drew back from the barrow, |
  of dark Maenefa the mountain;
A cusp still clasped him, a fluke yet fanged him, |
  entangled him, not quit utterly.
This was the prized, the desirable sight, |
  unsought, presented so easily,
Parted me leaf and leaf, divided me, |
  eyelid and eyelid of slumber.

Gerard Manley Hopkins (1844–1889)

Night

I love the silent hour of night,
  For blissful dreams may then arise,
Revealing to my charmèd sight
  What may not bless my waking eyes.

And then a voice may meet my ear,
  That death has silenced long ago;
And hope and rapture may appear
  Instead of solitude and woe.

Cold in the grave for years has lain
  The form it was my bliss to see;
And only dreams can bring again,
  The darling of my heart to me.

Anne Brontë (1820-1849)

Moonlight Night: Carmel

Tonight the waves march
In long ranks
Cutting the darkness
With their silver shanks,
Cutting the darkness
And kissing the moon
And beating the land's
Edge into a swoon.

Langston Hughes (1901–1967)

Midnight

Verses 1-4

There are sea and sky about me,
   And yet nothing sense can mark;
For a mist fills all the midnight
   Adding blindness to its dark.

There is not the faintest echo
   From the life of yesterday:
Not the vaguest stir foretelling
   Of a morrow on the way.

'Tis negation's hour of triumph
   In the absence of the sun;
'Tis the hour of endings, ended,
   Of beginnings, unbegun.

Yet the voice of awful silence
   Bids my waiting spirit hark;
There is action in the stillness,
   There is progress in the dark.

Louisa S. Bevington (1845–1895)

'Golden
Slumbers
kisse
your eyes'

Lullaby
Thomas Dekker

Midnight

The moon shines white and silent
On the mist, which, like a tide
Of some enchanted ocean,
O'er the wide marsh doth glide,
Spreading its ghost-like billows
Silently far and wide.

A vague and starry magic
Makes all things mysteries,
And lures the earth's dumb spirit
Up to the longing skies, –
I seem to hear dim whispers,
And tremulous replies.

The fireflies o'er the meadow
In pulses come and go;
The elm-trees' heavy shadow
Weighs on the grass below;
And faintly from the distance
The dreaming cock doth crow.

All things look strange and mystic,
The very bushes swell
And take wild shapes and motions,
As if beneath a spell –
They seem not the same lilacs
From childhood known so well.

The snow of deepest silence
O'er everything doth fall,
So beautiful and quiet,
And yet so like a pall, –
As if all life were ended,
And rest were come to all.

O wild and wondrous midnight,
There is a might in thee
To make the charmèd body
Almost like spirit be,
And give it some faint glimpses
Of immortality!

James Russell Lowell (1819-1891)

With Love from Midnight

When the day's mistakes
are too much to bear,
when everything feels
like devastation beyond repair,
remind yourself:
how mystical it is that everyday,
the clocks reset to 00.00
the reason they say
midnight is the witching hour
is because new day rises
from the ashes of the old,
embers breathe new life to its fire,
giving us a chance to mend,
a chance to restore
all that is broken
and what you thought was lost.

Nikita Gill (1987–)

This midnight hour
From *Midnight*

Men say, that in this midnight hour,
The disembodied have power
To wander as it liketh them,
By wizard oak and fairy stream,
 Through still and solemn places,
And by old walls and tombs, to dream,
 With pale, cold, mournful faces.
I fear them not; for they must be
Spirits of kindest sympathy,
Who choose such haunts, and joy to feel
The beauties of this calm night steal
Like music o'er them, while they woo'd
 The luxury of Solitude.

William Motherwell (1797–1835)

Fireflies in the Garden

Here come real stars to fill the upper skies,
And here on earth come emulating flies,
That though they never equal stars in size,
(And they were never really stars at heart)
Achieve at times a very star-like start.
Only, of course, they can't sustain the part.

Robert Frost (1874–1963)

Starlight
Verses 1–3

Mother, see! the stars are out,
Twinkling all the sky about;
Faster, faster, one by one,
From behind the clouds they run.
Are they hurrying forth to see
Children watching them like me?

"Oft I wonder, mother dear,
Why so many stars appear
Through the darkness every night,
With their little speck of light:
Hardly can a ray so small
Brighten up the world at all."

"Ah, you know not, little one,
Every dim star is a sun
To some planet-circle fair,
In its far-off home of air.
Rays that here so faint you call,
There in radiant sunshine fall."

Lucy Larcom (1824–1893)

On Stars

Stars are the nipples
of angels
pressed against the face
of heaven.

Grace Nichols (1950–)

Star Light, Star Bright

Star light, star bright,
First star I see tonight;
I wish I may, I wish I might
Have the wish I wish tonight.

English Nursery Rhyme, Anon

'Sleeping quietly. Love flows around me with its calm'

How Short a While
Mary Webb

Dark Days

On the darkest days,
I look at the stars,
and marvel at
the patchwork of time
staring back at me.

Not a single burst of starlight is the same age,
some of these stars
are born billions of years apart,
yet travel through time together
making this beautiful piece of art.

Sometime, somewhere,
these stars have already encountered
a better version of me
on her best day looking up at them
and thanking them for helping me see.

Nikita Gill (1987–)

When I heard the Learn'd Astronomer

When I heard the learn'd astronomer,
When the proofs, the figures, were ranged in columns
   before me,
When I was shown the charts and diagrams, to add,
   divide, and measure them,
When I sitting heard the astronomer where he
   lectured with much applause in the
    lecture-room,
How soon unaccountable I became tired and sick,
Till rising and gliding out I wander'd off by myself,
In the mystical moist night-air, and from time to
   time,
Look'd up in perfect silence at the stars.

Walt Whitman (1819–1892)

'Tis Moonlight Summer Moonlight

'Tis moonlight, summer moonlight
All soft and still and fair
The solemn hour of midnight
Breathes sweet thoughts everywhere

But most where trees are sending
Their breezy boughs on high
Or stooping low are lending
A shelter from the sky

And there in those wild bowers
A lovely form is laid
Green grass and dew-steeped flowers
Wave gently round her head

Emily Brontë (1818–1848)

Silver

Slowly, silently, now the moon
Walks the night in her silver shoon;
This ay, and that, she peers, and sees
Silver fruit upon silver trees;
One by one the casements catch
Her beams beneath the silvery thatch;
Couched in his kennel, like a log,
With paws of silver sleeps the dog;
From their shadowy cote the white breasts peep
Of doves in a silver-feathered sleep;
A harvest mouse goes scampering by,
With silver claws, and silver eye;
And moveless fish in the water gleam,
By silver reeds in a silver stream.

Walter de la Mare (1873–1956)

Impressions: II La Fuite de la Lune

To outer senses there is peace,
A dreamy peace on either hand,
Deep silence in the shadowy land,
Deep silence where the shadows cease.

Save for a cry that echoes shrill
From some lone bird disconsolate;
A corncrake calling to its mate;
The answer from the misty hill.

And suddenly the moon withdraws
Her sickle from the lightening skies,
And to her sombre cavern flies,
Wrapped in a veil of yellow gauze.

Oscar Wilde (1854–1900)

Hymn to the Moon
Written in July, in an Arbour

Thou silver deity of secret night,
   Direct my footsteps through the woodland shade;
Thou conscious witness of unknown delight,
   The Lover's guardian, and the Muse's aid!

By thy pale beams I solitary rove,
   To thee my tender grief confide;
Serenely sweet you gild the silent grove,
   My friend, my goddess, and my guide.

E'en thee, fair queen, from thy amazing height,
   The charms of young Endymion drew;
Veiled with the mantle of concealing night;
   With all thy greatness, and thy coldness too.

Lady Mary Wortley Montagu (1689-1762)

The moon was but a Chin of Gold

The Moon was but a Chin of Gold
A Night or two ago –
And now she turns Her perfect Face
Upon the World below –

Her Forehead is of Amplest Blonde –
Her Cheek – a Beryl hewn –
Her Eye unto the Summer Dew
The likest I have known –

Her Lips of Amber never part –
But what must be the smile
Upon Her Friend she could confer
Were such Her Silver Will –

And what a privilege to be
But the remotest Star –
For Certainty She take Her Way
Beside Your Palace Door –

Her Bonnet is the Firmament –
The Universe – Her Shoe –
The Stars – the Trinkets at Her Belt –
Her Dimities – of Blue.

Emily Dickinson (1830–1886)

Nightsong: City

Sleep well, my love, sleep well:
the harbour lights glaze over restless docks,
police cars cockroach through the tunnel streets

from the shanties creaking iron-sheets
violence like a bug-infested rag is tossed
and fear is imminent as sound in the wind-swung
  bell;

the long day's anger pants from sand and rocks;
but for this breathing night at last;
my land, my love, sleep well.

Dennis Brutus (1924–2009)

Gitanjali 24

If the day is done, if birds sing no more, if the wind
has flagged tired, then draw the veil of darkness
thick upon me, even as thou hast wrapt the earth
with the coverlet of sleep and tenderly closed the
petals of the drooping lotus at dusk.

From the traveller, whose sack of provisions is empty
before the voyage is ended, whose garment is
torn and dust-laden, whose strength is exhausted,
remove shame and poverty, and renew his life like a
flower under the cover of thy kindly night.

Rabindranath Tagore (1861–1941)

The Sleep
Verses 1 and 2

Of all the thoughts of God that are
Borne inward unto souls afar,
Along the Psalmist's music deep,
Now tell me if that any is,
For gift or grace, surpassing this –
'He giveth His beloved, sleep'?

What would we give to our beloved?
The hero's heart to be unmoved,
The poet's star-tuned harp, to sweep,
The patriot's voice to teach and rouse,
The monarch's crown, to light the brows? –
He giveth His belovèd, sleep.

Elizabeth Barrett Browning (1806–1861)

'Sleep well, my love, sleep well'

Nightsong: City
Dennis Brutus

Astrophil and Stella 39

Come sleep! O sleep, the certain knot of peace,
The baiting-place of wit, the balm of woe,
The poor man's wealth, the prisoner's release,
The indifferent judge between the high and low.
   With shield of proof shield me from out the press
Of those fierce darts despair at me doth throw:
O make in me those civil wars to cease;
I will good tribute pay, if thou do so.
   Take thou of me smooth pillows, sweetest bed,
A chamber deaf to noise and blind to light,
A rosy garland and a weary head:
And if these things, as being thine by right,
   Move not thy heavy grace, thou shalt in me,
   Livelier than elsewhere, Stella's image see.

Sir Philip Sidney (1554–1586)

All Through the Night

Sleep, my love, and peace attend thee,
   All through the night,
Guardian angels God will send thee,
   All through the night.
Soft the drowsy hours are creeping,
Hill and vale in slumber sleeping,
I my loving vigil keeping,
   All through the night.

Sir Harold Boulton (1859–1935)

Good Sport

I can't understand people who do not like sport,
I appreciate games of every sort,
For I find that when I'm trying to sleep,
Sports is much more effective than counting sheep.

Valerie Bloom (1956–)

Nuptial Sleep

At length their long kiss severed, with sweet smart:
  And as the last slow sudden drops are shed
  From sparkling eaves when all the storm has fled,
So singly flagged the pulses of each heart.
Their bosoms sundered, with the opening start
  Of married flowers to either side outspread
  From the knit stem; yet still their mouths, burnt
    red,
Fawned on each other where they lay apart.

Sleep sank them lower than the tide of dreams,
  And their dreams watched them sink, and slid
    away.
Slowly their souls swam up again, through gleams
  Of watered light and dull drowned waifs of day;
Till from some wonder of new woods and streams
  He woke, and wondered more: for there she lay.

D. G. Rossetti (1828–1882)

I know a bank where the wild thyme blows

From *A Midsummer Night's Dream*, Act II, scene i

I know a bank where the wild thyme blows,
Where oxlips and the nodding violet grows,
Quite over-canopied with luscious woodbine,
With sweet musk-roses, and with eglantine.
There sleeps Titania sometime of the night,
Lull'd in these flowers with dances and delight.

William Shakespeare (1564–1616)

Berceuse

Listen to Gieseking playing a Berceuse
of Chopin—the mothwing flutter
light as ash, perishable as burnt paper –

and sleep, now the furnaces of Auschwitz
are all out, and tourists go there.
The purest art has slept with turpitude,

we all pay taxes. Sleep. The day of waking
waits, cloned from the phoenix –
a thousand replicas in upright silos,

nurseries of the ultimate enterprise.
Decay will undo what it can, the rotten
fabric of our repose connives with doomsday.

Sleep on, scathed felicity. Sleep, rare
and perishable culprit. Imagining's no shutter
against the incorrigible absolute sunrise.

Amy Clampitt (1920-1994)

Serenade

(1250 AD)

With stars, with trailing galaxies,
   Like a white-rose bower in bloom,
Darkness garlands the vaulted skies,
   Day's ethereal tomb;
A whisper without from the briny west
   Thrills and sweetens the gloom;
Within, Miranda seeks her rest
   High in her turret-room.

Armies upon her walls encamp
   In silk and silver thread;
Chased and fretted, her silver lamp
   Dimly lights her bed;
And now the silken screen is drawn.
   The velvet coverlet spread;
And the pillow of down and snowy lawn
   Mantles about her head.

With violet-scented rain
   Sprinkle the rushy floor;
Let the tapestry hide the tinted pane,
   And cover the chamber door;
But leave a glimmering beam,
   Miranda belamour.
To touch and gild my waking dream,
   For I am your troubadour,

I sound my throbbing lyre.
    And sing to myself below;
Her damsel sits beside the fire
    Crooning a song I know;
The tapestry shakes on the wall,
    The shadows hurry and go,
The silent flames leap up and fall,
    And the muttering birch-logs glow.

Deep and sweet she sleeps,
    Because of her love for me;
And deep and sweet the peace that keeps
    My happy heart in fee!
Peace on the heights, in the deeps,
    Peace over hill and lea,
Peace through the star-lit steeps.
    Peace on the starlit sea.
Because a simple maiden sleeps
    Dreaming a dream of me!

John Davidson (1857–1909)

'The City grows quiet'

At Night
Sara Teasdale

A Portable Paradise

And if I speak of Paradise,
then I'm speaking of my grandmother
who told me to carry it always
on my person, concealed, so
no one else would know but me.
That way they can't steal it, she'd say.
And if life puts you under pressure,
trace its ridges in your pocket,
smell its piney scent on your handkerchief,
hum its anthem under your breath.
And if your stresses are sustained and daily,
get yourself to an empty room – be it hotel,
hostel or hovel – find a lamp
and empty your paradise onto a desk:
your white sands, green hills and fresh fish.
Shine the lamp on it like the fresh hope
of morning, and keep staring at it till you sleep.

Roger Robinson (1967–)

How Short a While

How short a while – eternities gone by –
It is since book and candle, half the night,
Consumed the hours, and in the first grey light
I turned and strove for slumber wearily:
But the sad past complained too mournfully,
And wept before me till the dawn grew white;
And the stark future, stripped of all delight,
Loomed up so near – I could but wake and sigh.

Now they are gone. I lie with ungirt will
And unlit candle, sleeping quietly.
Love flows around me with its calm and blessing;
I can but let it take me, and be still,
And know that you, beloved, though far from me,
All night are with me – comforting, caressing.

Mary Webb (1881–1927)

Sleep
From *Horace Book III, Ode I:IV*

Sleep is a God too proud to wait on Palaces,
   And yet so humble too, as not to scorn
The meanest Country Cottages:
   His Poppy grows among the Corn.
The *Halcyon Sleep* will never build his Nest
In any Stormy Breast.

Abraham Cowley (1618-1667)

The Country Bedroom

My room's a square and candle-lighted boat,
In the surrounding depths of night afloat;
My windows are the portholes, and the seas
The sound of rain on the dark apple-trees.

Seamonster-like beneath, an old horse blows
A snort of darkness from his sleeping nose,
Below, among drowned daisies. Far off, hark!
Far off one owl amidst the waves of dark.

Frances Cornford (1886–1960)

The Bedrooms

The bedrooms shall be
  gay with hints
of flowered Jacobean
  chintz,
and all the beds
  designed in pale
mahogany by
  Chippendale
(weed wide enough,
  as William* said,
to wrap a fairy in
  her bed).

*i.e. W. Shakespeare.

Humbert Wolfe (1885–1940)

The Singing Kettle

The singing Kettle and the purring Cat,
The gentle breathing of the cradled Babe,
The silence of the Mother's love-bright eye,
And tender smile answering its smile of Sleep.

Samuel Taylor Coleridge (1772-1834)

Early wrapt in slumber deep

Early wrapt in slumber deep
  Rest the serving-men;
Master, dame, and handmaids sleep
  Sound, at Bonny glen.

Time's dark stream in yonder vales
  Glides with shadowed flow;
O'er each latticed window falls
  A drapery, sweeping low.

While, within the house is spread
  Shade o'er weary eyes,
Screenless, in his out-door shed,
  A little herd-boy lies.

Splendid light from summer moon
  Falls on each green tree;
Soft as twilight, clear as noon,
  Smiles each dewy lea.

Water in the clear brook flows
  Fast, with trembling brightness;
By its side, the causeway shews
  A track of silver whiteness.

Charlotte Brontë (1816–1855)

Night Rain

What time of night it is
I do not know
Except that like some fish
Doped out of the deep
I have bobbed up bellywise
From stream of sleep
And no cock crow.
It is drumming hard here
And I suppose everywhere
Droning with insistent ardour upon
Our roof-thatch and shed
And through sheaves slit open
To lightning and rafters
I cannot quite make out overhead
Great water drops are dribbling
Falling like orange and mango
Fruits showered forth in the wind
Or perhaps I should say so
Much like beads I could in prayer tell
Then on string as they break
In wooden bowls and earthenware
Mother is busy now deploying
About our roomlet and floor
Although, it is so dark
I know her practiced step as

She moves her bins, bags and vats
Out of the run of water
That like ants filing out of the wood
Will scatter and gain possession
Of the floor. Do no tremble then
But turn brothers, turn upon your side
Of the loosening mats
To where the others lie.
We have drunk tonight of a spell
Deeper than the owl's or bat's
That wet of wings may not fly.
Bedraggled up on the *iroko*, they stand
Emptied of hearts, and
Therefore will not, stir, no, not
Even at dawn for then
They must scurry in to hide.
So we'll roll over our back
And again roll to the beat
Of drumming all over the land
And under its ample soothing hand
Joined to that of the sea
We will settle to sleep of the innocent and free.

John Pepper Clark (1935–2020)

The Candle

By my bed, on a little round table
The Grandmother placed a candle.
She gave me three kisses telling me they were three
  dreams
And tucked me in just where I loved being tucked.
Then she went out of the room and the door was
  shut.
I lay still, waiting for my three dreams to talk;
But they were silent.
Suddenly I remember giving her three kisses back.
Perhaps, by mistake, I had given my three little
  dreams.
I sat up in bed.
The room grew big, oh, bigger far than a church.
The wardrobe, quite by itself, as big as a house
And the jug on the washstand smiled at me:
It was not a friendly smile.
I looked at the basket-chair where my clothes lay
  folded:

The chair gave a creak as though it were listening
  for something.
Perhaps it was coming alive and going to dress in
  my clothes.
But the awful thing was the window:
I could not think what was outside.
No tree to be seen, I was sure,
No nice little plant or friendly pebbly path.
Why did she pull the blind down every night?
It was better to know.
I crunched my teeth and crept out of bed,
I peeped through a slit of the blind.
There was nothing at all to be seen.
But hundreds of friendly candles all over the sky
In remembrance of frightened children.
I went back to bed . . .
The three dreams started singing a little song.

Katherine Mansfield (1888–1923)

To Sleep

O soft embalmer of the still midnight,
   Shutting, with careful fingers and benign,
Our gloom-pleased eyes, embowered from the light,
   Enshaded in forgetfulness divine:
O soothest Sleep! if so it please thee, close
   In midst of this thine hymn, my willing eyes,
Or wait the 'Amen,' ere thy poppy throws
   Around my bed its lulling charities.
Then save me, or the passèd day will shine
Upon my pillow, breeding many woes;
   Save me from curious conscience, that still hoards
Its strength for darkness, burrowing like a mole;
   Turn the key deftly in the oilèd wards,
And seal the hushèd casket of my soul.

John Keats (1795–1821)

'the yellow half-moon large and low'

Meeting at Night
Robert Browning

Dreams

Thank God for dreams! I, desolate and lone,
　In the dark curtained night, did seem to be
The centre where all golden sun-rays shone,
　And, sitting there, held converse sweet with thee.
No shadow lurked between us; all was bright
　And beautiful as in the hours gone by,
I smiled, and was rewarded by the light
　Of olden days soft beaming from thine eye.
Thank God, thank God for dreams!

I thought the birds all listened; for thy voice
　Pulsed through the air, like beat of silver wings.
It made each chamber of my soul rejoice
　And thrilled along my heart's tear-rusted strings.
As some devout and ever 7yprayerful nun
　Tells her bright beads, and counts them o'er and
　　o'er,
Thy golden words I gathered, one by one,
　And slipped them into memory's precious store.
Thank God, thank God for dreams!

My lips met thine in one ecstatic kiss.
  Hand pressed in hand, and heart to heart we sat.
Why even now I am surcharged with bliss –
  With joy supreme, if I but think of that.
No fear of separation or of change
  Crept in to mar our sweet serene content.
In that blest vision, nothing could estrange
  Our wedded souls, in perfect union blent.
Thank God, thank God for dreams!

Thank God for dreams! when nothing else is left.
  When the sick soul, all tortured with its pain,
Knowing itself forever more bereft,
  Finds waiting hopeless and all watching vain,
When empty arms grow rigid with their ache,
  When eyes are blinded with sad tides of tears,
When stricken hearts do suffer, yet not break,
  For loss of those who come not with the years –
Thank God, thank God for dreams!

Ella Wheeler Wilcox (1850–1919)

Castles in the Air

My thoughts by night are often filled
   With visions false as fair:
For in the past alone I build
   My castles in the air.

I dwell not now on what may be:
   Night shadows o'er the scene:
But still my fancy wanders free
   Through that which might have been.

Thomas Love Peacock (1785–1866)

What did I dream?

What did I dream? I do not know—
   The fragments fly like chaff.
Yet, strange, my mind was tickled so
   I cannot help but laugh.

Pull the curtains close again,
   Tuck me grandly in;
Must a world of wonder wane
   Because birds begin

Complaining in a fretful tone,
   Rousing me from sleep:
The finest entertainment known,
   And given rag-cheap?

Robert Graves (1895-1985)

The Dream
Lines 1–10

Believe me, this was true last night,
  Tho' it is false today
  – A. M. F. Robinson

A fair dream to my chamber flew:
Such a crowd of folk that stirred,
Jested, fluttered; only you,
You alone of all that band,
Calm and silent, spake no word.
Only once you neared my place,
And your hand one moment's space
Sought the fingers of my hand;
Your eyes flashed to mine; I knew
All was well between us two.

Amy Levy (1861–1889)

Last night as I lay gazing with shut eyes

Last night as I lay gazing with shut eyes
      Into the golden land of dreams,
I thought I gazed adown a quiet reach
  Of land and water prospect,
      Whose low beach
Was peopled with the now subsiding hum
Of happy industry – whose work is done.

And as I turned me on my pillow o'er,
I heard the lapse of waves upon the shore,
Distinct as it had been at broad noonday,
And I were wandering at Rockaway.

Henry David Thoreau (1817–1862)

The Dream

Dear love, for nothing less than thee
Would I have broke this happy dream,
   It was a theme
For reason, much too strong for phantasy,
Therefore thou waked'st me wisely; yet
My dream thou brok'st not, but continued'st it;
Thou art so true that thoughts of thee suffice,
To make dreams truths, and fables histories;
Enter these arms, for since thou thought'st it best,
Not to dream all my dream, let's act the rest.

As lightning, or a taper's light,
Thine eyes, and not thy noise waked me;
   Yet I thought thee
(For thou lov'st truth) an angel, at first sight;
But when I saw thou saw'st my heart,
And knew'st my thoughts, beyond an angel's art,
When thou knew'st what I dreamt, when thou
  knew'st when
Excess of joy would wake me, and cam'st then,
I must confess, it could not choose but be
Profane, to think thee any thing but thee.

Coming and staying showed thee, thee,
But rising makes me doubt, that now
   Thou art not thou.
That love is weak where fear's as strong as he;
'Tis not all spirit, pure, and brave,
If mixture it of fear, shame, honour have.
Perchance as torches, which must ready be,
Men light and put out, so thou deal'st with me,
Thou cam'st to kindle, goest to come; then I
Will dream that hope again, but else would die.

John Donne (1572–1631)

At Night

Love said "Lie still and think of me,"
   Sleep, "Close your eyes till break of day,"
But Dreams came by and smilingly
   Gave both to Love and Sleep their way.

Sara Teasdale (1884–1933)

'O Sleep, the certain knot of peace'

Astrophil and Stella 39
Sir Philip Sidney

To Every Thing There is a Season
King James Bible, *Book of Ecclesiastes III*, verses i–viii

To everything there is a season,
and a time to every purpose under the heaven.
A time to be born, and a time to die:
a time to plant, and a time to pluck up that which is
  planted.
A time to kill, and a time to heal:
a time to break down, and a time to build up.
A time to weep, and a time to laugh:
a time to mourn, and a time to dance.
A time to cast away stones,
and a time to gather stones together:
a time to embrace, and a time to refrain from
  embracing.
A time to get, and a time to lose:
a time to keep, and a time to cast away.
A time to rend, and a time to sew:
a time to keep silence, and a time to speak.
A time to love, and a time to hate:
a time of war, and a time of peace.

A Summer Thought

I often think that all those vast desires
   For purer joys, that thrill the human heart,
Vague yearnings such as solitude inspires,
   That nameless something silence can impart,

Could after all be quenched by simple things,
   Whose spirits dwell within the wide-eyed flowers,
Or haunt deep glades, where scent of primrose clings
   About the garments of the passing hours.

Radclyffe Hall (1880–1943)

Nightsong

Silvery in the moonlight night
The river of my mind flows
To the nightsong of the truly great
Entombed in the caves of history
At heroes' acre. The music
Crescending through the valley
Of ghost towns and stabbed villages
Will come down to settle on our hearts
Like dew on leaves, tears for those
Who surrendered their lives at the altar
Leaving in us an eternal flame.

Hopewell Seyaseya

The Lake Isle of Innisfree

I will arise and go now, and go to Innisfree,
And a small cabin build there, of clay and wattles
  made;
Nine bean-rows will I have there, a hive for
  the honey-bee,
And live alone in the bee-loud glade.

And I shall have some peace there, for peace comes
  dropping slow,
Dropping from the veils of the morning to where
  the cricket sings;
There midnight's all a glimmer, and noon a purple
  glow,
And evening full of the linnet's wings.

I will arise and go now, for always night and day
I hear lake water lapping with low sounds by the
  shore;
While I stand on the roadway, or on the pavements
  grey,
I hear it in the deep heart's core.

W. B. Yeats (1865–1930)

‘Night shadows o'er the scene’

Castles in the Air
Thomas Love Peacock

Ode on Solitude

Happy the man whose wish and care
  A few paternal acres bound,
Content to breathe his native air,
      In his own ground.

Whose herds with milk, whose fields with bread,
  Whose flocks supply him with attire,
Whose trees in summer yield him shade,
      In winter fire.

Blest, who can unconcern'dly find
  Hours, days, and years slide soft away,
In health of body, peace of mind,
      Quiet by day,

Sound sleep by night; study and ease,
  Together mixt; sweet recreation;
And Innocence, which most does please
      With meditation.

Thus let me live, unseen, unknown,
  Thus unlamented let me die,
Steal from the world, and not a stone
      Tell where I lie.

Alexander Pope (1688–1744)

At Night
To W. M.

Home, home from the horizon far and clear,
  Hither the soft wings sweep;
Flocks of the memories of the day draw near
  The dovecote doors of sleep.

Oh, which are they that come through sweetest light
  Of all these homing birds?
Which with the straightest and the swiftest flight?
  Your words to me, your words!

Alice Meynell (1847-1922)

Serenity

The smiling sea
And dunes and sky
Dream; and the bee
Goes dreaming by.

In heaven's field
Moon's scimitar
Is drawn to shield
One dreaming star.

The dreaming flowers
And lovers nod.
Serene these hours –
Serene is God.

John Galsworthy (1867–1933)

All Shall be Well

From *Revelations of Divine Love,* The Thirteenth
Revelation

'Often I wondered why by the great foreseeing
wisdom of God the beginning of sin was not
hindered: for then, methought, all should have been
well.'

. . . .

And thus our good Lord answered to all the
questions and doubts that I might make, saying full
comfortably: I may make all thing well, I can make
all thing well, I will make all thing well, and I shall
make all thing well; and thou shalt see thyself that
all manner of thing shall be well.

Julian of Norwich (1342–c. 1430)
Edited by Grace Warwick (1855–1932)

Up-Hill

Does the road wind up-hill all the way?
  Yes, to the very end.
Will the day's journey take the whole long day?
  From morn to night, my friend.

But is there for the night a resting-place?
  A roof for when the slow dark hours begin.
May not the darkness hide it from my face?
  You cannot miss that inn.

Shall I meet other wayfarers at night?
  Those who have gone before.
Then must I knock, or call when just in sight?
  They will not keep you standing at that door.

Shall I find comfort, travel-sore and weak?
  Of labour you shall find the sum.
Will there be beds for me and all who seek?
  Yea, beds for all who come.

Christina Rossetti (1830-1894)

At the mid hour of night

At the mid hour of night when stars are weeping,
 I fly
To the lonely vale we lov'd when life shone warm in
 thine eye;
  And I think that if spirits can steal from the region
   of air,
  To revisit past scenes of delight; thou wilt come to
   me there,
And tell me our love is remember'd, even in the sky!

Then I'll sing the wild song it once was such rapture
 to hear,
When our voices, commingling breath'd like one on
 the ear,
  And, as Echo far off through the vale my sad orison
   rolls,
  I think, oh my love! 'tis thy voice from the kingdom
   of souls;
Faintly answering still the notes which once were
 so dear.

Thomas Moore (1779–1852)

'With paws of silver sleeps the dog'

Silver
Walter de la Mare

In Silence

I wondered why
Grandmother and Grandpapa
could sit
in Silence
on the front porch

She smoked a cigarette
He didn't
Sitting on the swing
in silence

I washed the dishes
and cleaned up
the kitchen
trying to figure
out why they sat
in Silence

Then I got to be
my own age
with my own desk
and my own person

and I understood

Nikki Giovanni (1943–)

Leisure

What is this life, if full of care,
We have no time to stand and stare.

No time to stand beneath the boughs
And stare as long as sheep or cows.

No time to see, when woods we pass,
Where squirrels hide their nuts in grass.

No time to see, in broad daylight,
Streams full of stars like skies at night.

No time to turn at Beauty's glance,
And watch her feet, how they can dance.

No time to wait till her mouth can
Enrich that smile her eyes began.

A poor life this, if full of care,
We have no time to stand and stare.

W. H. Davies (1871-1940)

'Thank
God
for
dreams!'

Dreams
Ella Wheeler Wilcox

At Night

We are apart; the city grows quiet between us,
  She hushes herself, for midnight makes heavy
    her eyes,
The tangle of traffic is ended, the cars are empty,
  Five streets divide us, and on them the moonlight
    lies.

Oh are you asleep, or lying awake, my lover?
  Open your dreams to my love and your heart
    to my words.
I send you my thoughts – the air between us is laden,
  My thoughts fly in at your window, a flock of
    wild birds.

Sara Teasdale (1884–1933)

The Hosanna of Small Mercies

Blink of green to greet the day.
What more can one ask of a leaf?

Blessing of a bird's octaves.
What more can one ask of a beak?

Breath of morning's first coffee.
What more can one ask of a bean?

Embrace of musk from old books.
What more can one ask of a shelf?

The hosanna of small mercies.
The salutation of self to self.

John Agard (1949–)

Index of Poets

Index of First Lines

My bed is like a little boat 40
My room's a square and candle-lighted boat 108
My thoughts by night are often filled 120

Night, ambushed in the darkling wood 66
November woods are bare and still 30–1
Now weary labourers perceive, well-pleased 12

O love, you so fear the dark 67
O! once again good night! 53
O soft embalmer of the still midnight 116
Of all the thoughts of God that are 94
'Often I wondered why by the great foreseeing 136
On the darkest days 85

Queene and huntresse, chaste and faire 68

Rest – rest -four little letters, one short word 45

She sits beside: through four low panes of glass 38
Silvery in the moonlight night 130
Sing to us, cedars; the twilight is creeping 58
Sleep is a God too proud to wait on Palaces 107
Sleep, my love, and peace attend thee 97
Sleep well, my love, sleep well 92
Sleeping sea, how calm you seem 62
Slowly, silently, now the moon 88

Acknowledgements

As always, a huge thank you to Hatchards, at Piccadilly, St Pancras and Cheltenham for looking after my books so well and, in particular, to Hatchards Piccadilly for tolerating the author in their midst. Thanks also Gemma Doyle for thinking of the original idea and last, but definitely not least, to my wonderful editors Nicola Newman and Magda Simões-Brown and everyone at Batsford who helps with these anthologies.

About the Editor

Jane McMorland Hunter has compiled anthologies for Batsford and the National Trust including collections on gardening, nature, food, friendship, books, London, England and the First World War. She also writes nature, gardening, cookery and craft books and works at Hatchards Bookshop in Piccadilly. At various times she has also worked as a gardener, potter and quilter. She lives in London in a house which is overflowing with books, with a small garden, which is overflowing with plants.

Sources

First published in the United Kingdom
in 2024 by
Batsford
43 Great Ormond Street
London
WC1N 3HZ

An imprint of B. T. Batsford Holdings Limited

ISBN 978-1-84994-947-7

A CIP catalogue record for this book is available from the
British Library.

10 9 8 7 6 5 4 3 2 1

Reproduction by Rival Colour Ltd, UK
Printed and bound by Elma Basim, Turkey

This book can be ordered direct from the publisher at
www.batsfordbooks.com, or try your local bookshop.

MIX
Paper from
responsible sources
FSC® C164814